Charles Dibdin

A Collection of Songs, Selected from the Works of Mr. Dibdin

Charles Dibdin

A Collection of Songs, Selected from the Works of Mr. Dibdin

ISBN/EAN: 9783744665162

Printed in Europe, USA, Canada, Australia, Japan

Cover: Foto ©Thomas Meinert / pixelio.de

More available books at **www.hansebooks.com**

A COLLECTION

OF

SONGS,

SELECTED FROM THE WORKS OF

Mr. DIBDIN.

TO WHICH ARE ADDED,

THE NEWEST AND MOST FAVOURITE

AMERICAN PATRIOTIC SONGS.

Let there be Mufic, let the Mafter touch
The fprightly String. and foftly breathing Flute.

———Ev'n Age itfelf is cheer'd with Mufic;
It wakes a glad remembrance of our youth,
Calls back paft joys, and warms us into tranfport!

Rowe.

If to be merry's to be wife, to be wife is to be merry.

PHILADELPHIA :

PRINTED BY J. BIOREN FOR H. & P. RICE,
AND SOLD BY J. RICE, BALTIMORE.
1799.

DIBDIN's

SELECTED SONGS.

SONG—IN THE WEDDING RING.

I saw what seem'd a harmlefs child,
  With wings and bow,
And afpect mild,
Who fobb'd, and figh'd, and pin'd,
  And begg'd I would fome boon beftow
On a poor little boy ftone blind.

Not aware of the danger, I inftant comply'd,
  When he drew from his quiver a dart,
    Cry'd
' My power you fhall know,'
Then he levelled his bow,
  And wounded me right in the heart.

BALLAD—IN THE DESERTER.

THERE was a miller's daughter
  Liv'd in a certain village,
Who made a mighty flaughter:
  For I'd have you to know
  Both friend and foe,
  The clown and the beau,
  She always laid low;
And her portion, as I underftand,
Was three acres of land,
  Befides a mill,
  That never ftood ftill,
  Some fheep and a cow,
  A harrow and plough,
And other things for tillage:
What d'ye think of my miller's daughter?

A

This miller's pretty daughter
  Was a damsel of such fame sir,
That knights and squires sought her;
  But they soon were told
  That some were too bold,
  And some too cold,
  And some too old;
And she gave them to understand
That, though they were grand,
  She'd never be sold:
For says Betty, says she,
  Since my virtue to me
  Is dearer than gold,
Let 'em go from whence they came sir.
What d'ye think of my miller's daughter?

But when the miller's daughter
  Saw Ned, the morrice-dancer,
His person quickly caught her;
  For who so clean
  Upon the green
  As Ned was seen,
  For her his queen:
Then blithe as a king,
His bells he'd ring,
  And dance, and sing,
  Like any thing:—
  Says he, ' My life,
  ' Woot be my wife?'
A blush, and yes, was Betty's answer.
What d'ye think of my miller's daughter?

BALLAD—IN THE WATERMAN.

TWO youths for my love are contending in vain;
  For, do all they can,
Their suff'rings I rally, and laugh at their pain;
  Which, which is the man
That deserves me the most? Let me ask of my heart,
Is it Robin, who smirks, and who dresses so smart?
Or Tom, honest Tom, who makes plainness his plan?
  Which, which is the man?

Indeed to be prudent, and do what I ought,
  I do what I can;

Yet furely papa and mamma are in fault;
  To a different man
They, each, have advifed me to yield up my heart,
Mamma praifes Robin, who dreffes fo fmart:
Papa honeft Tom, who makes plainnefs his plan :
  Which, which is the man?
Be kind then, my heart, and but point out the youth,
  I'll do what I can
His love to return, and return it with truth;
  Which, which is the man?
Be kind to my wifhes, and point out, my heart,
Is it Robin, who fmirks, and who dreffes fo fmart?
Or Tom, honeft Tom, who makes plainnefs his plan?
  Which, which is the man?

BALLAD—IN THE WATERMAN.

AND did you not hear of a jolly young waterman,
Who at Black friar's bridge ufed for to ply ;
And he feather'd his oars with fuch fkill and dexterity,
Winning each heart, and delighting each eye
He look'd fo neat, and row'd fo fteadily,
The maidens all flock'd in his boat fo readily,
And he ey'd the young rogues with fo charming an air,
That this waterman ne'er was in want of a fare.

What fights of fine folks he oft row'd in his wherry,
'Twas clean'd out fo nice, and fo painted withal ;
He was always firft oars when the fine city ladies
In a party to Ranelagh went, or Vauxhall
And oftentimes would they be giggling and leering,
But 'twas all one to Tom, their jiking and jeering,
For loving or liking he little did care.
For this waterman ne'er was in want of a fare.

And yet but to fee how ftrangely things happen,
As he row'd along, thinking of nothing at all,
He was ply'd by a damfel fo lovely and charming,
That fhe fmil'd, and fo ftraitway in love he did fall.
And would this young damfel but banifh his forrow,
He'd wed her to-night, before to-morrow,
And how fhould this waterman ever know care,
When he's married, and never in want of a fare.

BALLAD—IN THE WATERMAN.

THEN farewel my trim-built wherry,
  Oars, and coat, and badge farewel;
Never more at Chelfea ferry,
  Shall your Thomas take a fpell.

But to hope and peace a ftranger,
  In the battle's heat I'll go,
Where expofed to every danger,
  Some friendly ball may lay me low.

Then, may-hap, when homeward fteering,
  With the news my meffmates come,
Even you, the ftory hearing,
  With a figh-may cry poor Tom!

BALLAD—IN THE WATERMAN.

INDEED, Mifs, fuch fweethearts as I am,
  I fancy you'll meet with but few,
To love you more true I defy them,
  I always am thinking of you.

There are maidens would have me in plenty,
  Nell, Cicely, Prifcilla, and Sue,
But inftead of all thefe were there twenty,
  I never fhould think but of you.

Falfe hearts all your money may fquander,
  And only have pleafure in view,
Ne'er from you a moment I'll wander,
  Unlefs to get money for you.

The tide, when 'tis ebbing and flowing,
  Is not to the moon half fo true,
Nor my oars to their time when I'm rowing,
  As my heart, my fond heart is to you.

BALLAD—IN THE COBLER.

'TWAS in a village, near Caftlebury,
  A cobler and his wife did dwell;
And for a time no two fo merry,
  Their happinefs no tongue can tell.

But to this couple, the neighbours tell us,
  Something did happen that caus'd much ftrife,
For going to a neighb'ring alehoufe,
  The man got drunk and beat his wife.

But though he treated her fo vilely,
  What did this wife, good creature do?
Kept fnug, and found a method flily
  To wring his heart quite through and through:

For Dick the tapfter and his mafter,
  By the repert that then was rife,
Were both in hopes, by this difafter,
  To gain the cobler s pretty wife.

While things went on to rack and ruin,
  And all their furniture was fold,
She feem'd to approve what each was doing,
  And got from each a purfe of gold.

So when the cobler's cares were over,
  He fwore to lead an alter'd life,
To mind his work, ne'er be a rover,
  And love no other than his wife.

BALLAD—IN THE SERAGLIO.

THE world's a ftrange world, child, it muft be confeft,
  We all of diftrefs have our fhare;
But fince I muft ftruggle to live with the reft,
  By my troth 'tis no great matter where.
We all muft put up with what fortune has fent,
  Be therefore one's lot poor or rich,
So there is but a portion of eafe and content,
  By my troth 'tis no great matter which.

A living's a living, and fo there's an end;
  If one honeftly gets juft enow,
And fomething to fpare for the wants of a friend,
  By my troth 'tis no great matter how.
In this world about nothing we bufy'd appear;
  And I've faid it again and again,
Since quit it one muft, if ones confcience be clear,
  By my troth 'tis no great matter when.
A 2

RONDEAU—IN THE SERAGLIO.

Blow high, blow low, let tempeſts tear,
  The main maſt by the board ;
My heart, with thoughts of thee, my dear,
  And love well-ſtor'd,
Shall brave all danger, ſcorn all fear,
  The roaring winds, the raging ſea,
    In hopes on ſhore
    To be once more
Safe moor'd with thee.

Aloft while mountains high we go,
  The whiſtling winds that ſcud along,
And the ſurge roaring from below,
  Shall my ſignal be—
  To think on thee.
  And this ſhall be my ſong.
    Blow high, blow low, &c.

And on that night when all the crew
  The mem'ry of their former lives,
O'er flowing cans of flip renew,
  And drink their ſweethearts and their wives,
I'll heave a ſigh, and think on thee ;
And, as the ſhip rolls through the ſea,
The burthen of my ſong ſhall be
  Blow high, &c.

BALLAD—IN THE SERAGLIO.

THE little birds, as well as you,
  I've mark'd with anxious care,
How free their pleaſures they purſue,
  How void of every care.
But birds of various kinds you'll meet,
  Some conſtant to their loves :
Are chatt'ring ſparrows half ſo ſweet
  As tender cooing doves ?

Birds have their pride, like human kind,
  Some on their notes preſume,

Some on their form, and fome you'll find
Fond of a gaudy plume.
Some love a hundred; fome you'll meet
Still conftant to their loves;
Are chatt'ring fparrows half fo fweet
As tender, cooing doves?

SONG—IN POOR VULCAN.

VENUS now no more behold me,
But an humble village dame,
Coarfe and homely trappings fold me,
And Miftrefs Maudlin is my name.

Yet here no lefs is paid that duty
Ever due to Venus's worth,
Not more infenfible of beauty
Than gods in heaven, are men on earth.

BALLAD—IN POOR VULCAN.

THAT nature's every where the fame,
Each paffing day difcovers;
For that in me
Some charms they fee,
Behold me, though a country dame,
Leading a crowd of lovers.

My fporting fquire to keep at bay
The courfe I'll double over,
Whilft he, intent
On a wrong fcent,
Shall always find me ftole away
When he cries ' Hark to cover.'

With new-coin'd oaths, my grenadier
May think to ftorm and blufter,
And fwear by Mars,
My eyes are ftars,
That light to love —he'll foon find here
Such ftuff will ne'er pafs mufter.

Thus will I ferve thofe I diftruft,
Firft laugh at, then refufe 'em;

But, ah! not fo
My fhepherd Joe?
He like Adonis look'd, when firft
I prefs'd him to my bofom.

—<···<··<>··<>·· ⊜ ⊜ ⊜ ··>··>···<>··

BALLAD—IN POOR VULCAN.

THE moment Aurora peep'd into my room,
I put on my cloaths, and I call'd to my groom;
And, my head heavy ftill, from the fumes of laft night,
Took a bumper of brandy to fet all things right;
And now were well faddled Fleet, Dapple, and Gray,
Who feem'd longing to hear the glad found hark away.

Will Whiftle by this had uncoupled his hounds,
Whofe extacy nothing could keep within bounds;
Firft forward came Jowler, then Scentwell, then Snare,
Three better ftaunch harriers ne'er ftarted hare;
Then Sweetlips, then Driver, then Staunch, and then Tray,
All ready to open at hark, hark away.

'Twas now by the clock about five in the morn,
And we all gallop'd off to the found of the horn;
Jack Gater, Bill Babler, and Dick at the gun,
And by this time the merry Tom Fairplay made one,
Who, while we were jogging on blithfome and gay,
Sung a fong, and the chorus was—Hark, hark away.

And now Jemmy Lurcher had every bufh beat,
And no figns of madam, nor trace of her feet;
Nay, we juft had began our hard fortunes to curfe,
When all of a fudden out ftarts miftrefs Pufs;
Men, horfes, and dogs all the glad call obey,
And echo was heard to cry—Hark, hark away.

The chafe was a fine one, fhe took o'er the plain,
Which fhe doubled, and doubled, and doubled again;
Till at laft fhe to cover return'd out of breath,
Where I and Will Whiftle were in at the death;
Then in triumph for you I the hare did difplay,
And cry'd, to the horns my boys, hark, hark away.

—<>··—<>·· ⊜ ⊜ ⊜ ··<>··—<> ·

BALLAD—IN POOR VULCAN.

COME all ye gem'men volunteers,
Of glory who would fhare,

And leaving with your wives your fears,
  To the drum head repair;
Or to the noble ferjeant Pike,
  Come, come, without delay,
  You'll enter into prefent pay,
My lads the bargain ftrike.
A golden guinea and a crown,
Befides the Lord knows what renown,
  His majefty the donor,
    And if you die,
    Why then you lie
Stretch'd on the bed of honor.

Does any 'prentice work too hard,
  Fine cloaths would any wear,
Would any one his wife difcard,
  To the drum head repair.
    Or to the, &c.

Is your eftate put out to nurfe,
  Are you a caft-off heir,
Have you no money in your purfe,
  To the drum head repair.
    Or to the, &c.

BALLAD—IN POOR VULCAN.

COME, every man now give his toaft,
  Fill up the glafs, I'll tell you mine,
Wine is the miftrefs I love moft,
  This is my toaft—now give me thine.

Well faid my lad, ne'er let it ftand,
  I give my Chloe, nymph divine,
My love and wine go hand in hand ;—
  This is my toaft—now give me thine.

Fill up your glaffes to the brink,
  Hebe let no one dare decline,
'Twas Hebe taught me firft to drink :—
  This is my toaft—now give me thine.

Gem'men I give my wife, d'ye fee;
  May all to make her bleft combine,
So fhe be far enough from me ;—
  This is my toaft, now give me thine;

Let conſtant lovers at the feet
Of pale-fac'd wenches ſigh and pine,
For me the firſt kind girl I meet
Shall be my toaſt—now give me thine.

You toaſt your wife, and you your laſs,
My boys, and welcome; here's the wine,
For my part, he who fills my glaſs
Shall be my toaſt—now give me thine.

Spirit, my lads, and toaſt away,
I have ſtill one with yours to join;
That we may have enough to pay:
This is my toaſt—now give me thine.

BALLAD—IN POOR VULCAN.

MADAM, you know my trade is war,
And what ſhould I deny it for?
Whene'er the trumpet ſounds from far,
I long to hack and hew;
Yet madam credit what I ſay,
Were I this moment call'd away,
And all the troops drawn in array,
I'd rather ſtay with you.

Did drums and ſprightly trumpets ſound,
Did Death and Carnage ſtalk around,
Did dying horſes bite the ground,
Had we no hope in view;
Were the whole army loſt in ſmoke,
Were they the laſt words that I ſpoke,
I'd ſay, and dam'me if I joke,
I'd rather ſtay with you.

Did the foe charge us front and rear,
Did e'en the braveſt face appear
Impreſs'd with ſigns of mortal fear,
Though never veteran knew
So terrible and hot a fight,
Though all my laurels it ſhould blight,
Though I ſhould looſe ſo fine a fight,
I'd rather ſtay with you.

DUET.

JOE.

WHEN Serjeant Belfwagger, that mafculine brute,
One day had been drinking, to fwear a recruit,
He kifs'd you, I faw him, or elfe may I die,
And you cruel Maudlin, ne'er once cry'd O fie!

Again, when the fquire had come home from the chafe,
You receiv'd him, O Gods, with a fmile on your face,
Henceforth, then, my fheep harum fkarum may run,
For Maudlin is faithlefs, and I am undone.

MAUDLIN.

Ah, Joe! you're a good one; one day in my place—
My hufband at home—I was forced to fend Grace:
I know for a truth, which you cannot gainfay,
You touzled her well on a cock of new hay.

Nay, fwore you'd be hers—and, what is worfe yet,
That you only lov'd me juft for what you could get;
As for charms then I ne'er will believe I have one;
For Joey is faithlefs, and I am undone.

JOE.

Will you know then the truth on't? I touz'd her I own,
Though I rather by half would have left it alone;
But I did it to fee if you jealous would prove,
For that, people fay, is a fure fign of love.

MAUDLIN.

And for me, if the fquire faid foft things in my ear,
I fuffer'd it, thinking he'd call for ftrong beer;
And as to the ferjeant, 'tis always a rule,
One had better be kifs'd, than be teaz'd—by a fool.

BALLAD—IN THE QUAKER.

I LOCK'D up all my treafure,
I journied many a mile,
And by my grief did meafure
The pafling time the while.

My bufinefs done and over,
    I haften'd back back amain,
Like an expecting lover,
    To view it once again.

But this delight was ftifled,
    As it began to dawn :
I found the cafket rifled,
    And all my treafure gone.

SONG—IN THE QUAKER.

WOMEN are Will o' th' Wifps 'tis plain,
The clofer they feem, ftill the more they retire ;
    They teaze you, and jade you,
    And round about lead you,
    Without hopes of fhelter,
    Ding dong, helter fkelter,
'Through water and fire ;
    And, when you believe every danger and pain
    From your heart you may banifh,
And you're near the poffeffion of what you defire,
    That inftant they vanifh,
    And the devil a bit can you catch them again.

By fome they're not badly compared to the fea,
Which is calm and tempeftuous within the fame hour,
Some fay they are Sirens, but, take it from me,
They're a fweet race of angels o'er man that has pow'r,
    His perfon, his heart, nay his reafon to feize,
    And lead the poor devil wherever they pleafe.

BALLAD—IN THE QUAKER.

A Kernel from an apple's core
One day on either cheek I wore,
Lubin was plac'd on my right cheek,
That on my left did Hodge befpeak ;

Hodge in an inftant dropt to ground,
Sure token that his love's unfound,
But Lubin nothing could remove,
Sure token his is conftant love.

Laft May I fought to find a fnail,
That might my lover's name reveal,
Which finding, home I quickly fped
And on the hearth the embers fpread;
When, if my letters I can tell,
I faw it mark a curious L:
O may this omen lucky prove,
For L's for Lubin and for love.

RONDEAU—IN THE QUAKER.

While the lads of the village fhall merrily ah,
  Sound their tabors, I'll hand thee along,
And I fay unto thee, that merrily ah,
  Thou and I will be firft in the throng.

Juft then, when the youth who laft year won the dow'r,
  And his mate fhall the fports have begun,
When the gay voice of glad nefs refounds from each bow'r,
  And thou long'ft in thy heart to make one,
      While the lads, &c.
Thofe joys that are harmlefs what mortal can blame?
  'Tis my n axim that youth fhould be free;
And to prove that my words and my deeds are the fame,
  Believe thou fhalt prefently fee,
      While the lads, &c.

BALLAD—IN ROSE AND COLIN.

I loft my poor mother
  When only a child,
And I fear'd fuch another,
  So gentle and mild,
Was not to be found:
      B

But I saw my miftake,
    For fcarce was fhe gone,
    But I prov'd I had mother and father in one :
And though at this minute he makes my heart ach,
There's not fuch another fearch all the world round.

        I'd reach'd my teens fairly,
            As blithe as a bee,
        His care, late and early,
            Being all to pleafe me :
        No one thing above ground
    Was too good for his Rofe ;
    At wake, or at fair,
    I was dreft out fo gaily, lord, people would ftare,
And I fay it again, though he's peevifh, God knows,
There's not fuch another, fearch all the world round.

        But love, who, they tell us,
            Does many ftrange things,
        Makes all the world jealous,
            And mad—even kings
        They fay he can wound.
    This love is the fore :—
    Since Colin came here,
    This father fo kind is a father fevere ;
Yet ftill will I fay, though he fcolds more and more,
There's not fuch another, fearch all the world round.

BALLAD—IN ROSE AND COLIN.

HERE's all her geer, her wheel, her work;
    Thefe little bobbins to and fro,
How oft I've feen her fingers jerk,
    Her pretty fingers, white as fnow.
Fach object to me is fo dear,
    My heart at fight on't throbbings goes;
'Twas here fhe fat her down, and here
    She told me fhe was Colin's Rofe.

This poefy for her when fhe's drefs'd,
    I've brought, alas! how happy I,
Could I be, like thefe flowers, carefs'd,
    And, like them, on her bofom die.

The violet and pink I took,
And every pretty flower that blows;
The rose too, but how mean twill look
When by the side of my sweet Rose.

━◆┅┅◆━ ⬬ ⬬ ⬬ ┅◆┅┅◆┅

BALLAD—IN ROSE AND COLIN.

━━━━━

There was a jolly shepherd lad,
    And Colin was his name,
And all unknown to her old dad,
    He sometimes to see Peggy came—
    The object of his flame.
One day of his absence too secure,
    Her father thunder'd at the door,
When, fearing of his frown,
    Says she, 'dear love the chimney climb;'
    'I can't,' cries he, 'there is not time
'Besides, I should tumble down.'

What could they do, ta'en unawares?
    They thought, and thought again;
In closets underneath the stairs
    To hide himself 'twere all in vain,
    He'd soon be found, 'twere plain :
'Get up the chimney, love yo must,'
    Cry'd she, 'or else the door he'll burst,
    'I would not for a crown;'
Young Colin seeing but this shift,
E'en mounted up—Peg lent a lift,
    And cry'd; 'don't tumble down.'

With throbbing heart, now to the door,
    Poor Peggy runs in haste ;
Thinking to trick her father sure;
    But haste, the proverb says, makes waste,
    Which proverb's here well plac'd.
Her father scolded her his best,
    Call'd names, and said, among the rest,
    'Pray have you seen that clown?'
She scarce had time to answer no,
When all over black as a crow,
    Poor Colin tumbled down.

BALLAD—IN ROSE AND COLIN.

EXCUSE me, pray ye do, dear neighbour,
  But Rofe, you know, and I
Have oft partook one fport or labour,
  While you have pleas'd ftood by.
And fince from little children playing
  You've kindly called me fon,
I thought to Rofe I might be faying
  ' Good day,' and no harm done.

When you and father gravely counted,
  One morning in the barn,
To how much in a day it mounted
  That both of us could earn,
Since then you down the law were laying,
  And calling me your fon,
I thought to Rofe I might be faying
  ' Good day,' and no harm done.

BALLAD—IN ANNETTE AND LUBIN.

YOUNG, and void of art or guile,
  From ill intention free,
If love I've cherifh'd all this while,
  It came in fpight of me.
When you've to me, and I've to you,
  Try'd who could kindeft prove,
If that was love—what then to do
  To fly from this fame love ?

When abfent from you I have mourn'd,
  And thought each hour a fcore ;
When on a fudden you returned,
  I've thrill'd with joy all o'er ;
They fay 'twas love—I thought 'twas you
  Had made my heart thus move ;
Alas what can a poor girl do,
  To fly from this fame love ?

To every thing that you can afk,
  What fhould I fay but yes ?

It is because I like the task,
I freely grant each kiss.
You're all to me—I'm all to you—
This truth our deaths would prove,
Were we to part :—What then to do
To fly from this same love ?

DUET--IN ANNETTE AND LUBIN.

BAILIFF.

THEY tell me you listen to all that he says ;
That each hour of the day you are full of his praise ;
That you always together your flocks lead to graze :
Is this true damsel?

ANNETTE.
Yes, Mister Bailly.

BAILIFF.
They tell me also you are so void of grace
As to brag that dear form, and that dear pretty face,
That young dog shall be welcome to kiss and embrace :
Is this true damsel ?

ANNETTE.
Yes, Mister Bailly.

BAILIFF.
The neighbours all say, though I credit them not,
They have heard you declare that, content with your lot,
Any king you'd refuse for that lont and a cot :
Is this true damsel?

ANNETTE.
Yes, Mister Bailly.

BAILIFF.
But one thing I vow frights me out of my life,
'Tis allow'd on all hands, that is, barring the strife,
That you both live together just like man and wife :
Is this true damsel?

ANNETTE.
Yes, Mister Bailly.
B 2

DUET—IN ANNETTE AND LUBIN.

LUBIN.

'Tis true that oft, in the fame mead,
We both have led our flocks to feed,
Where by each other's fide we've fat;

ANNETTE.

Alas! there was no harm in that,

LUBIN.

'Tis true for thee this cot I rofe,
Where thou tak'ft pleafure to repofe;
For which I found the greeneft plat:

ANNETTE.

Alas! there was no harm in that.

LUBIN.

'Tis true when tired thou fain would'ft reft,
And thy dear lips to mine I've prefs'd,
Thy breath, fo fweet! I've wonder'd at:

ANNETTE.

Alas! there was no harm in that.

LUBIN.

Ah, but 'tis true, when thou haft flept,
Clofer and clofer have I crept;
And while my heart went pit-a-pat—

ANNETTE.

Alas! there was no harm in that.

BALLAD—IN ANNETTE AND LUBIN.

A PLAGUE take all fuch grumbling elves,
    If they will rail, fo be it;
Becaufe we're happier than themfelves,
    They can't endure to fee it.
For me, I never fhall repine,
    Let whate'er fate o'ertake us;
For love and Annette fhall be mine,
    Though all the world forfake us.

Then, dear Annette, regard them not,
The hours shall pass on gaily,
In spite of every snare and plot
Of that old doating Bailly.
No, never, Annette, thou'lt repine,
Let whate'er fate o'ertake us;
For love and Lubin shall be thine,
Though all the world forsake us.

BALLAD—IN ANNETTE AND LUBIN.

MY Lord, and please you, he and I,
Morn, noon, and night, in every weather,
From little children, not this high,
In the same cottage liv'd together.

Our parents left me to his care,
Saying, let no one put upon her:
' No, that I won't,' says he, ' I swear;'
And he ne'er lies, and like your honour.

As I was saying, we grew up,
For all the world sister and brother,
One never had nor bit nor sup,
Unless it was partook by t'other:

And I am sure, instead of me,
Were it a duchess, he had won her;
He is so good, and I've, d'ye see,
A tender heart, ank like your honour.

But, woe is ours, now comes the worst,
To-day our sorrows are beginning,
What I thought love—oh, I shall burst—
That nasty Bailly says was sinning.

With Lubin, who, of all the bliss
I ever tasted is the donor,
I took delight to toy and kiss,
Till I'm with child, and like your honour.

BALLAD—IN THE CHELSEA PENSIONER.

BROTHER soldiers why cast down?
Never, boys, be melancholy:

You fay our lives are not our own,
  But therefore fhould we not be jolly?

This poor tenement, at beft,
  Depends on fickle chance: mean while,
Drink, laugh, and fing; and, for the reft,
  We'll boldly brave each rude campaign;
Secure, if we return again,
  Our pretty landlady fhall fmile.

Fortune his life and yours commands,
  And this moment, fhould it pleafe her.
To require it at your hands,
  You can but die, and fo did Cæfar.

Our fpan, though long, were little worth,
  Did we not time with joy beguile:
Laugh then the while you ftay on earth,
  And boldly brave, &c.

Life's a debt we all muft pay,
  'Tis fo much pleafure, which we borrow,
Nor need, if on a diftant day
  It is demanded, or to-morrow.

The bottle fays we're tardy grown,
  Do not the time and liquor fpoil,
Laugh out the little life you own,
  And boldly brave, &c.

BALLAD—IN THE CHELSEA PENSIONER.

SING the loves of John and Jean,
  Sing the loves of Jean and John;
John, for her, would leave a queen,
  Jean, for him, the noblett don.
She's his queen,
    He's her don;
John loves Jean,
    And Jean loves John.

Whate'er rejoices happy Jean,
  Is fure to burft the fides of John,
Does fhe, for grief, look thin and lean,
  He inftantly is pale and wan:
Thin and lean,
    Pale and wan,
John loves Jean.
    And Jean loves John.

'Twas the lily hand of Jean
Fill'd the glafs of happy John:
And, heavens! how joyful was fhe feen
When he was for a licenfe gone!
  Joyful feen,
    They'll dance anon,
  For John weds Jean,
    And Jean weds John.

John has ta'en to wife his Jean,
 Jean's become the fpoufe of John,
She no longer is his queen,
He no longer is her don.
  No more queen,
  No more don;
  John hates Jean,
  And Jean hates John.

Whatever 'tis that pleafes Jean,
  Is certain now to difpleafe John;
With fcolding they're grown thin and lean,
  With fpleen and fpite they're pale and wan.
  Thin and lean,
  Pale and wan,
  John hates Jean,
  And Jean hates John.

John prays heaven to take his Jean,
  Jean at the devil wifhes John;
He'll dancing on her grave be feen,
  She'll laugh when he is dead and gone.
  They'll gay be feen,
  Dead and gone.
  For John hates Jean,
  And Jane hates John.

BALLAD—IN THE CHELSEA PENSIONER.

WHEN thou fhalt fee his bofom fwelling,
  When foft compaffion's tear fhall ftart,
As my poor father's woes thou'rt telling,
  Come back and claim my hand and heart.

The caufe bleft eloquence will lend thee;
  Nay, hafte, and eafe my foul's diftrefs;
To judge thy worth, I'll here attend thee,
  And rate thy love by thy fuccefs.

BALLAD—IN THE CHELSEA PENSIONER.

'TWAS not her eyes, though orient mines
  Can boaſt no gem ſo bright that glows;
Her lips, where the deep ruby ſhines,
  Her cheeks, that ſhame the bluſhing roſe,

Nor yet her form, Minerva's mien,
  Her boſom, white as Venus' dove,
That made her my affection's queen,
  But 'twas alone her filial love.

The ruby lip, the brilliant eye,
  The roſy cheek, the graceful form,
In turn for commendation vie,
  And juſtly the fir'd lover charm :

But tranſient theſe—the charm for life,
  Which reaſon ne'er ſhall diſapprove,
Which truly ſhall enſure a wife,
  Faithful and kind, is filial love.

SONG—IN THE CHELSEA PENSIONER.

LET your courage boy be true t'ye,
Hard and painful is the ſoldier's duty;
  'Tis not alone to bravely dare,
    To fear a ſtranger,
    Each threat'ning danger,
  That whiſtles through the duſky air;
Where thund'ring jar
    Conflicting arms,
    All the alarms,
And dreadful havock of the war.

Your duty done, and home returning,
With ſelf-commended ardour burning,
    If this right pride
    Foes ſhould deride,
    And from your merit turn aſide,
Though than the war the conflict's more ſevere,
This is the trial you muſt learn to bear.

BALLAD—IN THE FRIENDLY TARS.

WHILE up 'he shrouds the sailor goes,
　Or ventures on the yard,
The landsman, who no better knows,
　Believes his lot is hard.

But Jack with smiles each danger meets,
　Casts anchor, heaves the log,
Trims all the sails, belays the sheets,
　And drinks his can of grog.

When mountians high the waves that swell
　The vessel rudely bear,
Now sinking in the hollow dell,
　Now quiv'ring in the air.
　　Bold Jack, &c.

When waves 'gainst rocks and quicksands roar
　You ne'er hear him repine,
Freezing near Greenland's icy shore,
　Or burning near the line.
　　Bold Jack, &c.

If to engage they give the word,
　To quarters all repair,
While splinter'd masts go by the board,
　And shot sing through the air.
　　Bold Jack, &c.

BALLAD—IN THE FRIENDLY TARS.

I sail'd in the good ship the Kitty,
　With a smart blowing gale and rough sea,
Left my Polly, the lads call so pretty,
　Safe here at an anchor, Yo Yea.

She blubber'd salt tears when we parted,
　And cry'd now be constant to me;
I told her not to be down hearted,
　So up went the anchor, Yo Yea.

And from that time. no worse nor no better,
　I've thought on just nothing but she;
Nor could grog nor flip make me forget her,
　She's my best bower anchor, Yo Yea.

When the wind whiftled larboard and ftarboard,
   And the ftorm came on weather and lee,
The hope I with her fhould be harbour'd .
   Was my cable and anchor, Yo Yea.

And yet, my boys, would you believe me,
   I returned with no rhino from fea,
Miftrefs Polly would never receive me,
   So again I heav'd anchor, Yo Yea.

BALLAD—IN THE FRIENDLY TARS.

IF 'tis love to wifh you near,
To tremble when the wind I hear,
Becaufe at fea you floating rove :
If of you to dream at night,
To languifh when you're out of fight,
If this be loving—then I love.

If, when you're gone, to count each hour,
To afk of every tender power
That you may kind and faithful prove;
If void of falfhood and deceit,
I feel a pleafure now we meet,
If this be loving—then I love.

To wifh your fortune to partake,
Determin'd never to forfake,
Though low in poverty we ftrove;
If, fo that me your wife you'd call,
I offer you my little all;
If this be loving—then I love.

BALDAD—IN THE FRIENDLY TARS.

Yet though I've no fortune to offer,
   I've fomething to put on a par;
Come then, and accept of my proffer,
   'Tis the kind honeft heart of a tar.

Ne'er let fuch a trifle as this is,
   Girls, be to my pleafure a bar,
You'll be rich, though 'tis only in kiffes,
   With the kind honeft heart of a tar.

Befides, I am none of your ninnies ;
  The next time I come from afar
I'll give you your lao full of guineas,
  With the kind, honeft heart of a tar.

Your lords, with fuch fine baby faces,
  That ftrut in a garter and ftar,
Have they, under their tambour and laces,
  The kind, honeft heart of a tar.

I've this here to fay, now, and mind it,
  If love, that no hazard can mar,
You are feeking, you'll certainly find it
  In the kind honeft heart of a tar.

―――◆◆◆―――

BALLAD—IN THE OLD WOMAN OF EIGHTY.

Come here ye rich, come here ye great,
  Come here ye grave, come here ye gay,
Behold our bleft, though humble fate,
  Who, while the fun fhines, make our hay.
The gay plum'd lady, with her ftate,
  Would fhe in courts a moment ftay.
Could fhe but guefs our happy fate,
  Who, while the fun fhines, make our hay.
Nature we love, and art we hate,
  And, blithe and cheerful as the day,
We fing, and blefs our humble fate,
  And, while the fun fhines, make our hay.
Hodge goes a courting to his mate,
  Who ne'er coquets, nor fays him nay,
But fhares content, an humble fate,
  And, while the fun fhines, they make hay.
The captain puts on board his freight,
  And cuts through waves his dangerous way,
But we enjoy a gentler fate,
  And, while the fun fhines, make our hay.
See Hodge, and Dick, and Nell, and Kate,
  In the green meadow frifk and play,
And own that happy is our fate,
  Who, while the fun fhines, make our hay.
Come then, and quit each glitt'ring bait,
  Simplicity fhall point the way
C

To us, who blefs our humble fate,
And, while the fun fhines, make our hay.

BALLAD—in the old woman of eighty.

HOW kind and how good of his dear majefty,
    In the midft of his matters fo weighty,
To think of fo lowly a creature as me,
    A poor old woman of eighty.

Were your fparks to come round me, in love with each charm,
    Says I, I have nothing to fay t'ye;
I can get a young fellow to keep my back warm,
    Though a poor old woman of eighty.

John Strong is as comely a lad as you'll fee,
    And one that will never fay nay t'ye;
I cannot but think what a comfort he'll be
    To me, an old woman of eighty.

Then fear not, ye fair ones, though long paft your youth,
    You'll have lovers in fcores beg and pray t'ye,
Only think of my fortune, who have but one tooth,
    A poor old woman of eighty.

BALLAD—in the touchstone.

PARENTS may fairly thank themfelves,
    Should love our duty mafter,
Checking his power, the fenfelefs elves
    But tie the knot the fafter.

To trick fuch dotards, weak and vain,
    Is duty and allegiance,
Whilft love, and all his pleafing train,
    To fly were difobedience.

As fickle fancy, or caprice,
    Or headlong whim, advifes,
Children, and all their future peace,
    Become the facrifice:

Then trick thefe dotards, weak and vain,
    'Tis duty and allegiance;
Whilft love, and all his pleafing tra'n,
    To fly were dif-bedience.

SONG—IN THE TOUCHSTONE.

THIS life is like a troubled fea,
Where, helm a-weather or a-lec,
The fhip will neither flay nor wear,
But drives, of every rock in fear ;
All feamanfhip in vain we try,
We cannot keep her fteadily,
But, juft as fortune's wind may blow,
The veffel's tofticated to and fro ;
Yet, come but love on board,
Our hearts with pleafure ftor'd,
No ftorm can overwhelm,
  Still blows in vain
  The hurricane,
While he is at the helm.

BALLAD—IN THE TOUCHSTONE.

MY name's Ted Blarney, I'll be bound,
And man and boy, upon this ground,
Full twenty years I've beat my round,
  Crying Vauxhall watch :
And as that time's a litt'e fhort,
With fome fmall folks that here refort,
'To be fure I have not had fome fport,
  Crying Vauxhall.watch.
Oh of pretty wenches dreft fo tight,
And macaronies what a fight,
Of a moonlight morn I've bid good night,
  Crying Vauxhall watch.
The lover cries no foul will fee,
  You are deceived my love, cries fhe,
Dare's that Irifh taef there—meaning me—
  Crying Vauxhall watch.
So they goes on with their amorous talk,
'Till they gently fteals to the dark walk,
While I fteps afide, no fport to balk,
  Crying Vauxhall watch.
    Oh of pretty wenches, &c.

BALLAD—IN THE WIVES' REVENGE.

CURTIS was old Hodge's wife,
For virtue none was ever fuch,
She led fo pure, fo chaſte a life,
Hodge faid 'twas vartue over much:
For fays fly old Hodge, fays he,
Great talkers do the leaſt d'ye fee.

Curtis faid if men were rude
She'd fcratch their eyes out, tear their hair;
Cry'd Hodge, I believe thou'rt wond'rous good,
However, let us nothing fwear.
 For fays, &c.

One night fhe dreamt a drunken fool
Be rude with her in fpight would fain;
She makes no more, but, with joint ftool,
Falls on her hufband might and main.
 Still fays, &c.

By that time fhe had broke his nofe,
Hodge made fhift to wake his wife;
Dear Hodge, faid fhe, judge by thefe blows,
I prize my vartue as my life.
 Still fays, &c.

I dreamt a rude man on me fell;
However I his project marr'd:
Dear wife, cried Hodge, 'tis mighty well,
But next time don't hit quite fo hard.
 For fays, &c.

At break of day Hodge crofs'd a ftile,
Near to a field of new-mown hay,
And faw, and curft his ftars the while,
Curtis and Numps in am'rous play.
Was'nt I right, fays Hodge, fays he,
Great talkers do the leaſt d'ye fee.

GLEE—IN THE WIVES' REVENGE.

YOUNG Paris was bleft juft as I am this hour,
When proud Juno offer'd him riches and power,
When ftately Minerva of war talk'd and arms,
When Venus beam'd on him a fmile full of charms.

Venus' charms gain'd the prize, what an idiot was he!
The apple of gold I'd have parted in three;
And, contenting them all by this witty device,
Given juno, and Pallas, and Venus a flice.

BALLAD—IN THE SHEPHERDESS OF THE ALPS.

WHEN jealous out of feafon,
When deaf and blind to reafon,
Of truth we've no belief;
With rage we're overflowing,
Nor why, nor wherefore knowing,
And the heart goes throb with grief.

But when the fit is over,
And kindnefs from the lover
Does every doubt deftroy,
Away fly thoughts alarming,
Each objea appears charming,
And the heart goes throb with joy.

BALLAD—IN THE SHEPHERDESS OF THE ALPS.

BY love and fortune guided,
I quit the bufy town;
With cot and fheep provided,
And veftments of a clown.

Thus have I barter'd riches
For a fhepherd's little ftock;
A crook to leap o'er ditches,
And well to climb each rock:
A faithful dog, my fteps to guide,
A fcrip and hautboy by my fide,
And my horn, to give the alarm,
When wolves would harm
My flock.

Ah, fay then, who can blame me?
For beauty 'tis I roam;
But, if the chafe fhould tame me,
Perhaps I may come home.
Till then I'll give up riches, &c.

BALLAD—IN THE SHEPHERDESS OF THE ALPS.

THE rifing fun Lyfander found,
  Shedding tears o'er Phillis' tomb,
Who fwore he ne'er would leave the ground,
  But pafs his life in that dear gloom.
Tearing his hair, the frantic youth
  Cry'd, food and raiment I deny;
And with my life fhall end my truth,
  For love of Phillis will I die.

The radient god made half his tour,
  The kine fought fhelter from his heat,
Which pafs'd within the cottage door,
  Where poor Lyfander drank and eat.
His dinner finifh'd, up he rofe,
  Stalk'd, fighing, filently and flow,
To where were hung his Sunday's clothes,
  Then took a walk to chafe his woe.

The fun to Thetis made his way,
  When, underneath a friendly fhade,
A fhepherd fung in accents gay,
  His paffion for a gentle maid.
O lovers, what are all your cares!
  Your fighs! your fufferings! tell me what!
To Daphne 'tis Lyfander fwears,
  And lovely Phillis is forgot.

SONG—IN THE TOUCHSTONE.

MY tears—alas! I cannot fpeak!
  Muft thank this goodnefs, fure, divine!
For had I words—words are too weak,
  Too poor to vent fuch thoughts as mine.
The fun, in its meridian heigh',
  Will gratitude like this infpire;
Whofe kindly heat and piercing light,
  We wonder at, and we admire.

BALLAD—IN THE SHEPHERDESS OF THE ALPS.

THE coy Paſtora Damon woo'd,
  Damon the witty and the gay;
Damon, who never fair purſu'd
  But ſhe became an eaſy prey.
Yet, with this nymph, his ev'ry power
  In vain he tries, no language moves;
Thus do we ſee the tender flower
  Shrink from the ſun whoſe warmth it loves.

Piqued at the little angry puſs,
  Cry'd he, ſhe ſets me all on fire!
Then plagues herſelf, and makes this fuſs,
  Only to raiſe her value higher.
For, that ſhe loves me every hour,
  Each moment ſome new inſtance proves:
Thus do we ſee the tender flower
  Shrink from the ſun, whoſe warmth it loves.

How to reſolve then? what reſource?
  By fair means ſhe will near come to;
What of a little gentle force?
  Suppoſe I try what that will do?
I know ſhe'll tears in torrents pour;
  I know her cries will pierce the groves:
Thus do we ſee the tender flower
  Shrink from the ſun, whoſe warmth it loves.

RONDEAU—IN THE SHEPHERDESS OF THE ALPS.

AH men! what ſilly things you are.
  To woman thus to humble,
Who, fowler like, but ſpreads her ſnare,
    Or, at her timid game
    Takes aim,
  Pop, Pop, and down you tumble.

She marks you down, fly where you will,
  Or'e clover, graſs, or ſtubble;
Can wing you, feather you, or kill,
  Juſt as ſhe takes the trouble.
    Ah men, &c.

Then fly not from us, 'tis in vain,
We know the art of setting,
As well as shooting, and can train
The shyest man our net in.
Ah men, &c.

BALLAD—IN THE SHEPHERDESS OF THE ALPS.

BRIGHT gems that twinkle from afar,
Planets, and every lesser star,
That darting each a downward ray,
Console us for the loss of day,
Begone! e'en Venus, who so bright,
Reflects her visions pure and white,
Quick disappear, and quit the skies,
For lo! the moon begins to rise!

Ye pretty warblers of the grove,
Who chant such artless tales of love,
The throstle, gurgling in his throat,
The linnet with his silver note,
The soaring lark, the whistling thrush,
The mellow blackbird, goldfinch, hush,
Fly, vanish, disappear, take wing,
The nightingale begins to sing.

BALLAD—IN THE SHEPHERDESS OF THE ALPS.

HERE sleeps in peace, beneath this rustic vase,
The tenderest lover a husband could prove;
Of all this distress, alas! I am the cause,
So much I ador'd him, heaven envied my love.
The sighs I respire ev'ry morn I arise,
The misery I cherish, the grief, and the pain,
The thousand of tears that fall from my eyes,
Are all the sad comforts for me that remain.

When, his colours display'd, honour call'd him to arms,
By tender persuasions I kept him away,
His glory forgetting for these fatal charms,
And to punish me he is deprived of the day.

Since when to his memory I've rais'd this sad tomb,
Where to join him, alas! I shall shortly descend;
Where sorrow, nor pain, nor affliction can come,
And where both my love and my crime shall have end.

BALLAD—IN HARLEQUIN FREEMASON.

IN all your dealings take good care,
Instructed by the friendly square,
To be true, upright, just, and fair,
   And thou a fellow-craft shalt be:
The level so must poise thy mind,
That satisfaction thou shalt find,
When to another fortune's kind :—
   ' And that's the drift of masonry.

The compass t'other two compounds,
And says, though anger'd on just grounds,
Keep all your passions within bounds,
   And thou a fellow craft shalt be.
Thus symbols of our order are
The compass, level, and the square ;
Which teach us to be just and fair :
   And that's the drift of masonry.

BALLAD—IN HARLEQUIN FREEMASON.

THE Sun's a free-mason, he works all the day,
   Village, city, and town to adorn;
     Then from labour at rest,
     At his lodge in the west,
Takes with good brother Neptune a glass on his way.
   Thence ripe for the fair,
   He flies from all care,
     To Dame Thetis' charms,
     Till rous'd from her arms
   By the morn.
So do we, our labour done,
     First the glass,
     And then the lass,
     And then

Sweet flumbers give frefh force
To run our courfe,
Thus with the rifing fun.

The courfe of the fun all our myfteries defines :
Firft mafonry rofe in the eaft,
Then, to no point confin'd,
His rays cheer mankind ;
Befides, who'll deny but he well knows the figus ?
The Grand Mafter he
Then of mafons fhall be,
Nor fhall ought the craft harm,
Till to fhine and to warm
He has ceas'd.
Then like him, our labour done, &c.

oo(|oo ooo(|oo ⬤ ⬤ ⬤ *oo(|oo ooo(|oo*

BALLAD—IN HARLEQUIN FREEMASON.

AT a jovial meeting of gods once on high,
Ere Bacchus was hatch'd from old Jupiter's thigh,
This one told his ftory, and that fung his fong,
And did what he could left the time fhould feem long.
Apollo read verfes, the Graces wreath'd flowers,
The Mufes of harmony fung forth the powers,
Bully Mars crack'd his joke, and fly Momus his jeft;
Yet their mirth wanted fomething to give it a zeft.

Said Jove, our affembly to-day's pretty full,
Yet, I don't know how 'tis, we are horridly dull;
We have all the ingredients that mirth fhould infpire,
But fome clay-born alloy damps our heavenly fire,
I have it—in this I'll a mixture inclofe
Of all the delights whence good fellowfhip flows,
And we'll tafte of its produce, for mirth's bad at heft
When there's any thing wanting to give it a zeft.

So faying, fo doing, he buried the fhrine,
Which quickly fprung up in the form of a vine,
The leaves broad and verdant, the fruit deepeft blue,
Whence a juice flow'd that health, love, or youth might
renew.
Its influence to feel, they came round it in fwarms,
Mars took draughts of courage, and Venus drank
charms ;
Momus fwallow'd bon mots, Cupid love—fo the reft,
While Jove, fpurning nectar, cry'd—This is the zeft.

BALLAD—IN HARLEQUIN FREEMASON.

HERE I was, my good masters, my name's Teddy Clinch,
My cattle are found, and I drives to an inch;
From Hyde Park to White Chapel I well know the town,
And many's the time I've took up and set down:
In short, in the bills I'll be bound for't there's not
A young youth who, like Teddy, can tip the long trot.

Oh the notions of life that I see from my box,
While faces of all kinds come about me in flocks;
The sot whom I drive home to sleep out the day,
The kind one who plies for a fare at the play;
Or, your gents of the law, there, who, four in a lot,
To Westminster Hall I oft tip the long trot.

My coach receives all, like the gallows and sea,
So I touch but my fair you know all's one to me;
The men of the gown, and the men of the sword,
A ma'am, or a gambler, a rogue, or a lord;
To wherever you're going I well know the spot,
And, do you tip a tizzy, I'll tip the long trot.

BALLAD—IN THE ISLANDERS.

THE ladies' faces, now a-days,
　　Are various as their humours,
And on complexions oft we gaze,
　　Brought home from the perfumer's.

Hid as it were beneath a cloak,
　　The beauty's false that wins you,
Then pardon me, by way of joke,
　　If I prefer my Dingy.

A handkerchief can rub away
　　Your roses and your lillies;
The more you rub, the more you may,
　　My Dingy dingy still is

Besides, her hair is black as jet,
　　Her eyes are gems from India;
Rail as you list then, I sha'l yet,
　　For joke's sake love poor Dingy.

BALLAD—IN THE ISLANDERS.

DID fortune bid me chufe a ftate
From all that's rich, and all that's great,
From all that oftentation brings,
The fplendor, pride, and pomp of kings;
Thefe gifts, and more, did fhe difplay,
With health, that felt not life's decay,
I'd fpurn with fcorn the ufelefs lot,
Were my Camilla's name forgot.

But did fhe for my fate affign,
That I fhould labour in a mine;
Or, with many wretches more,
In flavery chain me to an oar;
Or from the fight of men exiled,
Send me to a Siberian wild,
For this and more would fhe attone,
Were my Camilla all my own.

BALLAD—IN THE ISLANDERS.

WHEN Yanko dear fight far away,
    Some token kind me fend;
One branch of olive, for dat fay
    Me wifh de battle end.
The poplar tremble as him go,
    Say of dy life take care,
Me fend no laurel, for me know
    Of that him find him fhare.

De ivy fay my heart be true,
    Me droop fay willow tree,
De torn he fay me fick for you,
    De fun-flower tink of me.
Till laft me go, weep wid the pine,
    For fear poor Yanko dead;
He come, and I de myrtle twine,
    In chaplet for him head.

SONG—IN THE ISLANDERS.

I'LL mount the cliffs, I'll watch the coast,
  Anxious some welcome tidings soon to bear,
Nor let your fortitude be lost,
  Confiding still in honest Yanko's care,
Though to my comrades I'm untrue,
  Honour shall infidelity applaud,
And call in charity to you,
  My broken faith to them a pious fraud.

BALLAD—IN THE ISLANDERS.

ORRA no talk, no say fine word,
  No dress him, no look gay,
Vay little sing you hear yon bird,
  Him mate be gone away.
Orra tell true, she have no grace
  Of lady for him part,
Dare beauty all be in him face,
  But Orra in him heart.

Orra do little, all she do;
  Frogive, for she no gall,
To every ting she promise true,
  Love Yanko, and dat all.
    But Orra, &c.

BALLAD—IN THE ISLANDERS.

POOR Orra tink of Yanko dear,
  Do he be gone forever,
For he no dead, he still live here,
  And he from here go never.
Like on a sand me mark him face,
  De wave come roll him over,
De mark him go, but still the place
  'Tis easy to discover.

D

I fee fore now de tree de flower,
  He droop like Orra, furely,
And den by'm bye there'come a fhower,
  He hold him head up purely:
And fo fome time me tink me die,
  My heart fo fick he grieve me,
But in a lily time me cry
  Good deal, and dat relieve me.

SONG—IN THE ISLANDERS.

PASSION is a torrent rude,
Which rapid bears down every height,
  A turbulent, unruly flood,
Which with the ocean would unite.

  Reafon's a fountain, calm ferene,
Which, near gay fields, and laughing bow'rs,
  While it reflects th' enchanting fcene,
Is born among a bed of flowers.

BALLAD—IN THE ISLANDERS.

A BED of mofs we'll ftraight prepare,
  Where, near him gently creeping,
We'll pat his cheeks, and ftroke his hair,
  And watch him while he's fleeping.

Sweet flowers of every fcent and hue,
  Pinks, violets, and rofes,
And blooming hyacinths we'll ftrew,
  As fweetly he repofes.

And we'll with fond emotion ftart,
  And while, with admiration,
We foftly feel his fluttering heart,
  Partake its palpitation.

BALLAD—IN THE ISLANDERS.

COME, courage lads, and drink away,
A man upon his wedding day
Ought rarely well his part to play
  At Stingo, or October:

For, who would be that stupid elf
For whim, caprice, or love, or pelf,
To poison, hang, or drown himself,
    Or marry when he's sober.

For madam's will at nothing stops,
She must have balls, and routs, and fops,
And often ransack all the shops,
    In gay attire to robe her:
Then drink the day you take a wife,
As the last comfort of your life:
For, ever after, noise and strife
    Are sure to keep you sober.

BALLAD—INTENDED FOR THE QUAKER.

THOU'ST heard those old proverbs, ne'er lean on a rush,
A bird in the hand is worth two in the bush,
'Tis the money paid down that decides who's the winner,
Who waits upon fortune's ne'er sure of a dinner:
Out of sight out of mind, delaying breeds danger,
He ought to be cozen'd who trusts to a stranger·
Heaven take my friend, and the old one my brother,
Promising's one thing, performing another.

Much may fall out 'twixt the cup and the lip,
The builder's receipt's the best sail in the ship,
'Tis a good thing to lend, but a better to borrow,
Pay me to-day, and I'll trust you to-morrow.
Brag is a good dog, but hold-fast a better,
You may guess at a word when you know the first letter,
There's not the most fire where you see the most smother,
Promising's one thing, performing another.

BALLAD—IN THE MISCHANCE.

O THINK on the time when you came home at night,
And supp'd upon muscles, no lily more white,
When I u'ed to provide you with many a treat
Of as fine Melton oysters as ever were eat.
Now see what a change! all the muscles for me
May be trod under foot, or thrown into the sea;
My Joey is false! and the once sprightly tone
With which I cry'd oysters is sunk to a drone!

When the laft kit of falmon we fat down to broach,
And you told me your heart was as found as a roach,
How fweet was my temper ! what joys did I fell,
Little thinking you'd flip through my hands like an eel.
But my temper's now chang'd—I, that once was fo mild,
I was thought to be gentle and meek as a child,
So crufty am grown, I ne'er fpeak a word civil,
And my cuftomers fay I'm as crofs as the devil.

My ftall was fo clean, and my tubs were fo white,
They were perfectly—people would tell me—a fight:
I liften'd with joy when the folks told me fo,
For my ftall and my tubs were both fcower'd for Joe.
But now they're all dirty, neglected they lie,
I oft take them up, and as oft throw them by,
For his fake I pleafure in cleaning them found,
He has left me, and now they're as black as the ground.

BALLAD—IN PANDORA.

WHAT naughty things we women are,
  Who long for fruit forbidden ;
Though 'twere our bane, we cannot bear
  The leaft thing from us hidden.
But what we fee will we believe,
  Though ill on ill we're heaping,
Though to this day, from mother Eve,
  We have always paid for peeping.

Thus curious girls, urged by their youth,
  Thoughtlefs what they were doing,
Have falfhood found difguis'd like truth,
  And mafk'd like pleafure, ruin.
Inftead of fmiling, who muft grieve,
  Whofe joys are turn'd to weeping,
And who too late, like mother Eve,
  Find they have paid for peeping.

Should I to my defires give way,
  I may encounter forrow,
And that I think a good to-day,
  May prove an ill to-morrow.
Yet, cautious prudence, by your leave,
  The fecret's in my keeping;
I am weak woman, and, like Eve,
  Cannot refrain from peeping.

BALLAD—IN THE REASONABLE ANIMALS.

—*A Wolf who had been a Lawyer.*—

By roguery, 'tis true,
I opulent grew,
Juft like any other profeffional finner ;
An orphan, d'ye fee,
Would juft wafh down my tea,
And a poor friendlefs widow would ferve me for dinner.

I was, to be fure,
Of the helplefs and poor
A guardian appointed to manage the pelf ;
And I manag'd it well,
But how—fays you—tell ?
Why I let them all ftarve, to take care of myfelf.

With thefe tricks I went on
Till, faith fir, anon,
A parcel of ftupid, mean-fpirited fou's,
As they narrowly watch'd me,
Soon at my tricks catch'd me.
And, in their own words, haul'd me over the coals.'
In the pillory, that fate
For rogues, foon or late,
I ftood, for the fport of a difolute mob;
Till my neck Mafter Ketch
Was fo eager to ftretch,
That I gave the thing up as a dangerous job.

Now a wolf!—from their dams
I fteal plenty of lambs,
Pamper'd high, and well fed—an infatiable glutton—
In much the fame fphere
When a man, I move here,
Make and break laws at pleafure, and kill my own
mutton.
Then fince, for their fport,
No one here moves the court,
Nor am I amenable to an employer,
I fhall ever prefer,
With your leave, my good fir,
The life of a wolf to the life of a lawyer.

D 2

BALLAD—IN THE REASONABLE ANIMALS.

—A hog who had been an alderman—

FOR dainties I've had of them all,
At taverns, Lord Mayor's, and Guildhall,
Where the purveyors, nothing stingy,
    To fill the wallet,
    And pamper the palate,
Have rarities brought from India.

Then what signifies what one takes in,
For, when one's cram'd up to the chin,
Why, really, good friend to my thinking,
    If on venison and wines,
    Or on hogwash, one dines,
At last 'tis but eating and drinking.

Besides, I've no books I arrange,
Nor at two need I e'er go to change;
Have no business with note, bond, or tally,
    Nor need I, from any ill luck,
    Either bull, or a bear, or lame duck,
Ever fear waddling out of the alley.
    For dainties, &c.

BALLAD—IN THE REASONABLE ANIMALS.

—A bull who had been an Irishman—

IS'T my story you'd know?—I was Patrick Mulrooney,
    A jolman, and Ireland my nation,
To be sure I was not a tight fellow too, honey,
    Before my transmogrification.

I did not at all talk of flames and of darts,
To conquer the fair—the dear jewels!
And wid husbands, becase why I won their wives' hearts,
    I did not fight plenty of duels.
        Then arrah, bodder how you can,
            You'll ne'er persuade me, honey,
        For I shall always, bull or man,
            Be Patrick Mulrooney.

When at Almack's, or White's, or at Brookes's, or Boodle's,
  I've fat up all night in the morning,
'Mongft black legs, and coggers, and pigeons, and noodles,
  The calling to ufe I was born in:
To be fure many honeft gold guineas it yields,
  But, fince 'tis a fervice of danger,
I'm a better man now I'm a bull in the fields,
  To popping and tilting a ftranger.

BALLAD—IN LIBERTY-HALL.

WERE Patience kind to me
  Oh he de nos!
Far plyther than a coat I'd be,
  Oh he de nos!

Leap, fkip, and pound, would poor Ap Hugh,
And capriole, and caper too,
And frifk, and jump, and dance, look you,
  Oh he de nos!

But Patience very cruel is,
  Oh he de nos!
With jibes, and cheers, and mockeries,
  Oh he de nos!

Which makes to figh and fob Ap Hugh,
And whining, his fad fortune rue,
And grieve, and groan, and grunt, look you,
  Oh he de nos!

BALLAD—IN LIBERTY-HALL.

WHEN faintly gleams the doubtful day,
  Ere yet the dew drops on the thorn,
Borrow a luftre from the ray
  That tips with gold the dancing corn,
Health bids awake, and homage pay
  To him who gave another morn.
And, well with ftrength his nerves to brace,
Urges the fportfman to the chafe.

Do we purfue the timid hare,
  As trembling o'er the lawn fhe bounds?
Still of her fafety have we care,

While feeming death her fteps furrounds,
We the defencelefs creature fpare,
    And inftant flop the well taught hounds:
For cruelty fhould ne'er difgrace
The well-earn'd pleafure of the chafe.

Do we purfue the fubtle fox,
    Still let him breaks and rivers try,
Through marfhes wade, or climb the rocks,
    The deep-mouth'd hounds fhall following fly
And while he every danger mocks,
    Unpitied fhall the culprit die:
To quell this cruel, artful race,
Is labour worthy of the chafe.

Return'd, with fhaggy fpoils well ftor'd,
    To our convivial joys at night,
We toaft, and firft our country's lord,
    Anxious who moft fhall do him right;
The fair next crowns the focial board,
    Britons fhould love as well as fight—
For he who flights the tender race,
Is held unworthy of the chafe.

SONG—IN LIBERTY-HALL.

WHO to my wounds a balm advifes,
    But little knows what I endure;
The patient's pain to torture rifes
    When medicine's try'd, and fails to cure.

What can the wifeft counfel teach me,
    But fad remembrance of my grief?
Alas! your kindnefs cannot reach me,
    It gives but words—I afk relief.

BALLAD—IN LIBERTY-HALL.

JACK RATLIN was the ableft fea-man,
None like him could hand, reef, and fteer,
No dangerous toil but he'd encounter,
With fkill, and in contempt of fear:
In fight a lion—the battle ended,
Meek as a bleating lamb he'd prove;

Thus Jack had manners, courage, merit,
Yet did he figh, and all for love.

The fong, the jeft, the flowing liquor,
For none of thefe had Jack regard;
He, while his meffinates were caroufing,
High fitting on the pendant yard,
Would think upon his fair ones beauties,
Swear never from fuch charms to rove,
That truly he'd adore them living,
And, dying, figh—to end his love.

The fame exprefs the crew commanded
Once more to view their native land,
Among the reft, brought Jack fome tidings,
Would it had been his love's fair hand!
Oh fate—her death defac'd the letter,
Inftant her pulfe forgot to move,
With quiv'ring lips, and eyes uplifted,
He heav'd a figh—and dy'd for love!

GLEE—IN LIBERTY HALL.

WHAT if my pleafures fools condemn,
Becaufe I am not dull, like them,
Becaufe no minute I let pafs,
Unmark'd by a convivial glafs?
Or elfe retir'd from ftrife and noife,
I tempt the fair to fofter joys;
A mortal with a foul divine,
Alternate crown'd with love and wine.

Thefe fhall on earth my being fhare,
And when I'm gone, if in my heir
My fpirit live, let him not mourn,
But fee embofs'd upon my urn.
Bacchus and Venus in a wreath,
With this infcription underneath:
" This mortal had a foul divine,
" Alternate crow'd with love and wine."

BALLAD—IN LIBERTY-HALL.

WHEN fairies are lighted by night's filver queen,
And feaft in the meadow, or dance on the green,
My Lambkin afide lays his plough and his flail,

By yon oak to fit near me, and tell his fond tale.
And though I'm affur'd the fame vows were believed
By Patty and Ruth, he forfook and deceived,
Yet, fo fweet are his words, and like truth fo appear,
I pardon the treafon, the traitor's fo dear.

I faw the ftraw bonnet he bought at the fair,
The rofe-colour'd ribbon to deck Jenny's hair,
The fhoe-ties of Bridget, and ftill worfe than this,
The gloves he gave Peggy for ftealing a kifs.
All thefe did I fee, and with heart-rending pain,
Swore to part; yet I know, when I fee him again,
His words and his looks will like truth fo appear,
I fhall pardon the treafon, the traitor's fo dear.

BALLAD—IN LIBERTY HALL.

SEE the courfe throng'd with gazers, the fports are begun
The confufion but hear!—I'll bet you fir—done, done;
Ten thoufand ftrange murmurs refound far and near,
Lords, hawkers, and jockies, affail the tir'd ear :
While with neck like a rainbow, erecting his creft,
Pamper'd, prancing, and pleas'd, his head touching his
            breaft
Scarcely fnuffing the air, he's fo proud and elate,
The high-mettled racer firft ftarts for the plate.

Now renard's turn'd out, and o'er hedge and ditch rufh,
Hounds, horfes, and huntfmen, all hard at this brufh ;
They run him at length, and they have him at bay,
And by fcent and by view cheat a long tedious way :
While, alike born for fports of the field and the courfe,
Always fure to come thorough, a ftaunch and fleet horfe ;
When fairly run down, the fox yields up his breath,
The high-mettled racer is in at the death.

Grown aged, ufed up, and turn'd out of the ftud,
Lame, fpavin'd, and windgali'd, but yet with fome blood ;
While lowing poftillions his pedigree trace,
Tell his dam won the fweepftcakes, his fire gain'd that race ;
And what matches he won to the oftlers count o'er,
As they loiter their time at fome hedge ale houfe door,
While the harnefs fore galls, and the fpurs his fides goad,
The high-mettled racer's a hack on the road.

Till at laft, having labour'd, drudg'd early and late,
Bow'd down-by degrees, he bends on his fa e,
Blind, old, lean, and feeble, he tugs round a mill,
Or draws fand, till the fand of his hour-glafs ftands ftill :
And now, cold and lifelefs, expofed to the view,
In the very fame cart which he vefterday drew,
While a pitying crowd his fad relicks furrounds,
The high-mettled racer is fold for the hounds.

BALLAD—IN LIBERTY HALL.

DO falmonds love a lucid ftream ?
  Do thirfty fheep love fountains?
Do Druids love a doleful theine ?
  Or goats the craggy mountains ?
If it be true thefe things are fo,
  As truly fhe's my lovey,
  And os wit l yng carie I,
  Rooi fit dwyn de garie di,
As cin, dai, tree, pedwar, pimp, chwcck go
  The bells of Aberdovey.

Do keffels love a whifp of hay ?
  Do fprightly kids love prancing ?
Do curates crowdics love to play ?
  Or peafants morice dancing ?
  If it be true, &c.

BALLAD—IN THE BENEVOLENT TAR.

A PLAGUE of thofe mufty old lubbers,
  Who tell us to faft and to think,
And patient fall in with life's rubbers,
  With nothing but water to drink.
A can of good ftuff! had they twigg'd it,
'Twould have fet them for pleafure agog,
    And, fpight of the rules
    Of the fchools,
    The old fools
Would have all of 'em fwigg'd it,
And fwore there was nothing like grog.

My father when laſt I from Guinea
  Return'd, with abundance of wealth,
Cry'd Jack, never be ſuch a ninny
  To drink :—ſaid I—father your health.
So I ſhew'd him the ſtuff, and he twigg'd it,
And it ſet the old codger agog,
    And he ſwigg'd, and mother,
    And ſiſter, and brother,
And I ſwigg'd, and all of us ſwigg'd it,
And ſwore there was nothing like grog.

T'other day as the chaplain was preaching,
  Behind him I curiouſly ſlunk,
And while he our duty was teaching,
  As how we ſhould never get drunk,
I ſhew'd him the ſtuff, and he twigg'd it,
And it ſoon ſet his rev'rence agog.
    And he ſwigg'd, and Nick ſwigg'd,
    And Ben ſwigg'd, and Dick ſwigg'd,
And I ſwigg'd, and all of us ſwigg'd it,
And ſwore there was nothing like grog.

Then truſt me there's nothing like drinking,
  So pleaſant on this ſide the grave ;
It keeps the unhappy from thinking,
  And makes e'en they aliant more brave.
As for me, from the moment I twigg'd it,
The good ſtuff has ſo ſet me agog,
    Sick or well, late or early,
    Wind foully or fairly,
    Helm a-lee or a-weather,
    For hours together,
I've conſtantly ſwigg'd it,
And, dam'me, there's nothing like grog.

BALLAD—IN THE BENEVOLENT TAR.

WHAT argufies pride and ambition ?
Soon or late death will take us in tow ;
Each bullet has got its commiſſion,
And when our time's come we muſt go.

Then drink and ſing—hang pain and ſorrow,
The halter was made for the neck ;
He that's now live and luſty—to-morrow
Perhaps may be ſtretch'd on the deck.

Then drink and fing—hang pain and forrow,
The halter was made for the neck;
He that's now live and lully—to-morrow
Perhaps may be ftretch'd on the deck.

There was little Tom Linftock of Dover
Got kill'd, and left Polly in pain,
Poll cry'd, but her grief was foon over,
And then fhe got married again.
Then drink, &c.

Jack Junk was ill ufed by Bet Crocker,
And fo took to guzzling the ftuff,
Till he tumbled in old Davy's locker,
And there he got liquor enough.
Then drink, &c.

For our prize money then to the proctor,
Take of joy while 'tis going our freak;
For what argufies calling the doctor
When the anchor of life is apeak.
Then drink, &c.

BALLAD—IN THE BENEVOLENT TAR.

A Sailor's love is void of art,
Plain failing to his port, the heart,
He knows no jealous folly:
'Twere hard enough at fea to war
With boifterous elements that jar—
All's peace with lovely Polly.

Enough that, far from fight of fhore,
Clouds frown, and angry billows roar,
Still is he brifk and jolly:
And while caroufing with his mates,
Her health he drinks—anticipates
The fmiles of lovely Polly.

Should thunder on the horizon prefs,
Mocking our fignals of diftrefs,
E'en then dull melancholy,
Dares not intrude:—he braves the din,
In hopes to find a calm within
The fnowy arms of Polly.

E

BALLAD—IN THE MILK MAID.

SWEET dities would my Patty fing,
Old Chevy Chafe, God fave the King,
Fair Rofemy, and Sawny Scot,
Lilebularo, the Irifh Trot,
All thefe would fing my blue-ey'd Patty.
As with her pail fhe'd trudge along,
While ftill the burthen of her fong
My hammer beat to blue-ey'd Patty.

But nipping frofts and chilling rain
Too foon alas choak'd every ftrain ;
Too foon, alas! the miry way
Her wet fhod feet did fore difmay,
And hoarfe was heard my blue-ey'd Patty.
While I for very mad did cry ;
Ah could I but again, faid I,
Hear the fweet voice of blue-ey'd Patty!

Love taught me how—I work'd, I fung,
My anvil glow'd, my hammer rung,
Till I had form'd from out the fire,
To hear her feet above the mire,
An engine for my blue-ey'd Patty.
Again was heard each tuneful clofe,
My fair one on the patten rofe,
Which takes its name from blue-ey'd Patty.

BALLAD—IN HARVEST HOME.

As Dermot toil'd one fummer's day,
Young Shelah, as fhe fat behind him,
Fairly ftole his pipe away—
Oh den to hear how fhe'd deride him.
Where, poor Dermot is it gone,
Your lily lily loodle ?
They've left you nothing but the drone.
And that's yourfelf, you noodle.
Beum bum boodle, loodle lo,
Poor Dermot's pipe is loft and gone,
And what will the poor devil do ?

Fait, now I am undone and more,
Cry'd Dermot—ah will you be aefy?
Did not you ftale my heart before?
Is it you'd have a man run crazy?
I've nothing left me now to moan,
My lily lily loodle,
That ufed to chear me fo is gone—
Ah Dermot thou'rt a noodle.
Beum bum boodle, loodle lo,
My heart, and pipe, and peace are gone—
What next will cruel Shelah do?

But Shelah hearing Dermot vex,
Cry'd fhe, 'twas little Cupid mov'd me,
Ye fool to fteel it out of tricks,
Only to fee how much you lov'd me.
Come cheer thee Dermont, never moan,
But take your lily loodle,
And for the heart of you that's gone,
You fhall have mine, you noodle.
Beum bum boodle, loodle lo,
Shela's to church with Dermot gone,
And for the reft—what's dat to you.

BALLAD—IN CLUMP AND CUDDEN.

THIS, this my lad's a foldier's life,
He marches to the fprightly fife,
And in each town to fome new wife,
    Swears he'll be ever true;
He's here—he's there—where is he not?
Variety's his envied lot,
He eats, drinks, fleeps, and pays no fhot,
And follows the loud tattoo.

Call'd out to face his country's foes,
The tears of fond domeftic woes
He kiffes off, and boldly goes
'To earn of fame his due.
Religion, liberty, and laws,
Both his are, and his country's caufe—
For thefe, through danger, without paufe,
    He follows the loud tattoo.

And if at laft, in honour's wars,
He earns his fhare of danger's fcars,

Still he feels bold, and thanks his stars
  He's no worse fate to rue:
At Chelsea, free from toil and pain,
He wields his crutch, points out the slain,
And, in fond fancy, once again,
  Follows the loud tattoo.

BALLAD—IN TOM THUMB.

IS it little Tom Thumb that you mean, and his battles?
Arrah send him for playthings some whistles and rattles:
At the sight of a sword all his nerves would be quaking,
He fight! he kill giants! is it game you are making?
As well may you tell us that eagles fear larks,
That mice eat up lions, and sprats swallow sharks:
Then talk not of any such nonsense to me—
Wid your confounded boderum bumboodle liddle lee.

Tom Thumb! such a shrimp sure no eyes ever saw—
He handles his arms as a fly hugs a straw:
To be sure in the wars dangers certain to quit him,
For the taef's such a flea dare's no bullet can hit him.
And then as to courage, my jewel—hoot, hoot!
Arrah did not I find him chin deep in my boot?
Then talk not of any such nonsense to me,
Wid your confounded boderum bumboodle liddle lee.

Tom Thumb marry you!—musha honey he aefy,
Were it not for your sense, I should think you gone crazy:
Shall a fine stately ostrich thus wed a cock-sparrow?
'Twere a halberd stuck up by the side of an arrow—
Or a fly on a church, or a mountain and mouse,
Or a pismire that crawls by the side of a house:
Then talk not of any such nonsense to me,
Wid your confounded boderum, bumboodle liddle lee.

BALLAD.

THAT all the world is up in arms,
And talks of nought but Celia's charms,
That crowds of lovers near and far,
Come all to see this blazing star,

Is true—who has not heard on't.
But that fhe all at diftance keeps,
And that her virtue never fleeps—
I don't believe a word on't.

That for one lover had fhe ten,
In fhort, did fhe from all the men
Her homage due each day receive,
She has good fenfe, and, I believe,
Would never grow abfurd on't :
But for foft dalliance fhe'd refufe.
Some favourite from the crowd to chufe—
I don't believe a word on't.

That in the face of ftanders-by
She's modefty itfelf's no lie ;
That then were men rude things to fay,
'Twould anger her—oh I would lay
A bottle and a bird on't :
But to her bedchamber, d'ye fee,
That Betty has no private key
I don't believe a word on't.

BALLAD.

I Thought we were fiddle and bow,
    So well we in concert kept time,
But, to ftrike up a part bafe and low,
    Without either reafon or rhime :
What a natural was I fo foon
    With pleafure to quaver away !
For I'm humm'd, I think, now to fome tune,
    She has left me the piper to pay.

I plainly perceive fhe's in glee,
    And thinks I fhall be fuch a flat
As to fhake, but fhe's in a wrong key,
    For fhe never fhall catch me at that.
Whoe'er to the crotches of love
    Lets his heart dance a jig in his breaft,
'Twill a bar to his happinefs prove,
    And fhall furely deprive him of reft.

BALLAD.

I fing of a war fet on foot for a toy,
And of Paris, and Helen, and Hector, and Troy,
Where on women, kings, gen'rals, and coblers you ftumble,
And of mortals and gods meet a very ftrange jumble,
Sing didderoo bubberoo, oh my joy,
How fweetly they did one another deftroy!
Come, fill up your bumpers, the whifky enjoy,
May we ne'er fee the like of the fiege of Troy!

Menelaus was happy wid Helen his wife,
Except that fhe led him a devil of a life,
Wid dat handfome tafe Paris fhe'd toy and fhe'd p'ay,
Till they pack'd up their alls, and they both ran away.
    Sing didderoo, &c.

Agamemnon, and all the great chiefs of his houfe,
Soon took up the caufe of this hornified fpoufe,
While Juno faid this thing, and Venus faid that,
And the gods fell a wrangling they knew not for what.
    Sing didderoo, &c.

Oh den fuch a flaughter, and cutting of trotes,
And flaying of bullocks, and offering up goats!
Till the cunning Ulyffes, the Trojans to crofs,
Clapt forty fine fellows in one wooden horfe.
    Sing didderoo, &c.

Oh den for to fee the maids, widows, and wives,
Crying fome for their virtue, and fome for their lives;
Thus after ten years they'd defended their town,
Poor dear Troy in ten minutes was all burnt down!
    Sing didderoo, &c.

But to fee how it ended's the beft joke of all,
Scarce had wrong'd Menelaus afcended the wall,
But he blubb'ring faw Helen, and, oh ftrange to tell,
The man took his mare, and fo all was well.
    Sing didderoo, &c.

BALLAD.

I Sing Ulyffes, and thofe chiefs
Who, out of near a million,

So luckily their bacon fav'd
  Before the walls of Ilion.
Yankee doodle doodle doo,
  Black negro he get fumbo,
And when you come to our town
  We'll make you drunk with bumbo.

Who having taken, fack'd, and burnt,
  That very firft of cities,
Return'd in triumph, while the bards
  All ftruck up amorous ditties.
    Yankee doodle, &c.

The Cyclops firft we vifited,
  Ulyffes made him cry out,
For he eat his mutton, drank his wine,
  And then he pok'd his eye out.
    Yankee doodle, &c.

From thence we went to Circe's land,
  Who faith a girl of fpunk is,
For fhe made us drunk, and chang'd us all
  To affes, goats, and monkies.
    Yankee doodle, &c.

And then to hell and back again,
  Then where the Syrens Cara,
Swell cadence, trill, and fhake, almoft
  As well as Madam Mara.
    Yankee doodle, &c.

To fell Charibdis next, and then
  Where yawning Scylla grapples
Six men at once, and eats them all,
  Juft like fo many apples.
    Yankee doodle, &c.

From thence to where Apollo's bulls
  And fheep all play and fkip fo,
From whence Ulyffes went alone
  To the Ifland of Calypfo.
    Yankee doodle, &c.

And there he kifs'd, and toy'd, and play'd,
  "Tis true upon my life fir,
Till, having turn'd his miftrefs off,
  He's coming to his wife fir.
    Yankee doodle, &c.

G L E E.

WE, on the present hour relying,
  Think not of future, nor of past,
But seize each moment as 'tis flying,
  Perhaps the next may be our last.
Perhaps old Charon, at his wherry,
  This moment waits to waft us o'er;
Then charge your glasses, and be merry,
  For fear we ne'er should charge them more.

With brow austere, and head reclining,
  Let envy, age, and haggard care
Grow four, and at our joy repining,
  Blame pleasures which they cannot share.
Put round the glasses, and be jolly,
  In spight of all such idle stuff,
Whether 'tis wisdom or 'tis folly,
  'Tis pleasure boys, and that's enough.

BALLAD.

I'VE made to marches Mars descend,
Justice in jigs her scales suspend,
Magicians in gavots portend,
  And Furies black wigs bristle:
To prestos Pallas Ægis' blaze,
Snakes twist to fugues a thousand ways,
And Jove whole towns with lightning raze,
  At sound of the prompter's whistle.

I've made a sun of polish'd tin,
Dragons of wood, with ghastly grin,
A canvas sea, the which within
  Did leather Dolphins caper;
I've strung with packthread Orpheus' lyre,
Made sheep and oxen dance with wire,
And have destroyed, with painted fire,
  Grand temples of cartridge paper.

I've made a swain, his love asleep,
Chide warbling birds and bleating sheep,
While he himself did bawling keep,
  Like boatman at a ferry :

I've racks made that no blood could spill,
Foul poison that could do no ill,
And daggers queens and princes kill,
Who are alive and merry.

—◁—◁—◁—◁—❬❭❬❭❬❭—◁—▷—▷—

BALLAD.

WHEN last from the straights we had fairly cast anchor,
I went, bonny Kitty to hail,
With quintables stor'd, for our voyage was a spanker,
And bran new was every sail:
But I knew well enough how, with words sweet as honey,
They trick us poor tars of our gold,
And when the sly gipsies have finger'd the money,
The bag they poor Jack give to hold.

So I chafed her, d'ye see, my lads, under false colours,
Swore my riches were all at an end,
That I'd sported away all my good-looking dollars,
And borrow'd my togs of a friend:
Oh then had you seen her, no longer my honey,
'Twas varlet, audacious and bold,
Begone from my sight—now you've spent all your money
For Kitty the bag you may hold.

With that I took out double handfuls of shiners,
And scornfully bid her good bye,
'Twould have done your heart good had you then seen her
fine airs,
How she'd leer, and she'd fob, and she'd sigh;
But I stood well the broadside, while jewel and honey
She call'd me, I put up the gold,
And bearing away, as I fack'd all the money,
Left the bag for Ma'am Kitty to hold.

—◁—◁—◁—❬❭❬❭❬❭—◁—◁—

BALLAD—INTENDED FOR THE QUAKER.

THOU man of firmness turn this way,
Nor time by absence measure,
The sportive dance, the sprightly lay
Shall wake thee into pleasure:
Spite of thy formal outward man,
Thou'rt gay, as we shall prove thee;

Then cheer thee, laugh away thy fpan,
　And let the fpirit move thee.

None are more juft, more true, more fair,
　More upright in their dealings,
Than men of thy profeffion are,
　But are they without feelings ?
E'en now I know thy honeft heart
　Full forely doth reprove thee;
Be gay then, in our joy take part,
　And let the fpirit move thee.

BALLAD.

IN Paris, as in London,
Vice thrives, and virtue's undone;
Errors, paffions, want of truth,
Folly, in age as well as youth,
　Are things by no means rare,
But honeft ufurers, friends fincere,
And judges with their confcience clear,
　C'eft qu'on ne voit guere.

In Paris All things vary,
Sixteen and fixty marry;
Men prefuming on their purfe,
Heirs with their eftates at nurfe,
　Are things by no means rare:
But doctors who refufe a fee,
And wives and hufbands who agree,
　C'eft qu'on ne voit guere.

In Paris idle paffion
And folly lead the fafhion;
Attention paid to fhew and drefs,
Modeft merit in diftrefs,
　Are things by no means rare:
But friendfhip in farcaftic fneers,
And honefty in widow's tears,
　C'eft qu'on ne voit guere.

BALLAD.

BEHOLD the fairies' jocund band,
Who firm, though low of ftature,

'Gainſt giant vice ſha'l make a ſtand.
Pourtraying human nature.
We've characters of every mould,
All tempers, forms, and ſizes,
The grave, the gay, the young, the old,
Hid under quaint diſguiſes.
Then hey for the fairies, &c.

We have a prieſt who never ſwears,
But who is always ready
With money, or advice, or prayers,
To help the poor and needy.
Then hey for the fairies, &c.

A man and wife, who both on crutch
Are now obliged to hobble,
Who fifty years, or near as much,
Have never had a ſquabble.
Then hey for the fairies, &c.

A magiſtrate upright and wife,
To whom no brihe is given,
And who before two charming eyes
Can hold the balance even.
Then hey for the fairies, &c.

A learn'd phyſician of great ſkill,
All cures, like Galen, pat in,
Who never does his patients kill,
Take fees, or jabbers latin.
Then hey for the fairies, &c.

A country ſquire who hates the ſmell
Of Stingo and October,
A modern poet who can ſpell,
And a muſician ſober.
Then hey for the fairies, &c.

Away then, comrades, beat to arms,
Diſplay your ſportful banners,
Strike hard at vice, explore falſe charms,
And catch the living manners.
Then hey for the fairies, &c.

BALLAD.

CHAIRS to mend, old chairs to mend.
Like mine to botch is each man's fate,
Each toils in his vocation—

One man tinkers up the ſtate,
  Another mends the nation.
Your parſons preach to mend the heart,
  They cobble heads at college ;
Phyſicians patch with terms of art
  And latin want of knowledge.
But none for praiſe can more contend
    'Than I,
    Who cry
Old chairs to mend.

Your lawyer's tools are flaws and pleas ;
  They manners mend by dancing ;
Wigs are patches for degrees,
  And lovers uſe romancing :
Fortunes are mended up and made,
  Too frequently, with places—
With rouge, when their complexions fade,
  Some ladies mend their faces.
    But none for praiſe, &c.

BALLAD.

A Tinker I am,
  My name's Natty Sam,
From morn to night I trudge it ;
  So low is my fate,
  My perſonal eſtate
Lies all within this budget.
Work for the tinker ho, good wives,
  For they are lads of mettle—
Twere well if you could mend your lives,
  As I can mend a kettle.

  The man of war
  The man of the bar,
Phyſicians, prieſts, free-thinkers,
  That rove up and down
  Great London town,
What are they all but tinkers ?
  Work for the tinker, &c.

  Thoſe 'mong the great
  Who make the ſtate,

And badger the minority,
 Pray what's the end
 Of their work, my friend,
But to rivet a good majority?
 Work for the tinker, &c.
 This mends his name,
 That cobbles his fame,
That tinkers his reputation:
 And thus, had I time,
 I could prove in my rhyme,
Jolly tinkers of all the nation.
 Work for the tinker, &c.

BALLAD.

ART one of thofe mad wags, whofe brain
Intruder reafon can't contain,
Who are of fuch unruly minds,
They buffet waves, and fplit the winds;
In blanket robe, and crown of ftraw,
Who to mad fubjects deal mad law?
If this 'tis makes thy bofom fwell,
Hie demoniac to thy cell.

Or art thou drunk—a frenzy too,
One of that hair-brain'd, noify crew,
Who vigils keep at Bacchus' fhrine,
And drown good reafon in bad wine?
Every defire in life who think
Compris'd in a defire to drink!
If by this demon thou'rt poffeft,
Hie the good drunkard home to reft.

Or art in love, and fo gone mad?
Doft go with folded arms? art fad?
Doft figh? doft languifh? doft play pranks?
For which contempt is all thy thanks?
Doft pant? doft long for fome frail charms,
Devoted to another's arms?
Is this thy madnefs, ftupid elf?
Hie thee away and hang thyfelf.

F

62   DIBDIN'S SELECTED SONGS.

BALLAD—IN CLUMP AND CUDDEN.

WHEN in order drawn up, and adorn'd in his beft,
If my foldier appears with more grace than the reft,
If his gaiters are jet, his accoutrements fine,
If his hair's tied up tight, and his arms brightly fhine,
Let him turn, wheel, or face, march, kneel, ftoop, or ftand,
Anxious ftill to obey every word of command;
Erect like an arrow, or bending his knee,
'Tis not for the general, 'tis all to pleafe me.
If with fmoak and with duft cover'd over by turns,
To gain a fham height, or falfe baftion, he burns;
If, of danger in fpight, and regardlefs of fear,
He rufhes to fight when there's nobody near:
    In fhort, let him turn, &c.

BALLAD—IN CLUMP AND CUDDEN.

A Novice in love, and a ftranger to art,
As pure as my wifhes my unpractis'd heart;
When I rofe with the lark, and out-warbled the thrufh,
Free from falfhood or guile, for I knew not to blufh :
        Thofe paft days I deplore.
When innocence guarded my unfullied fame,
When to think, and to act, and commend were the fame ;
        When on my face,
        In artlefs grace,
Danc'd frolic fport and pleafure—now no more.
Ere I liften'd and lov'd, ere man fmil'd, and betray'd,
Ere by horror appall'd, and of confcience afraid ;
Loft to each fond delight that e'er woman adorn'd,
By a hard judging world look'd at, pity'd, and fcorn'd,
        Thofe paft joys I deplore :
Thofe joys, ere by man's artful treachery forfook,
Which, guiltlefs and pleafed, with the world I partook;
        When on my face,
        With artlefs grace,
Danc'd frolic fport and pleafure—now no more.

DUET—IN CLUMP AND CUDDEN.

PLATOON.

SAY Fanny, wilt thou go with me?
Perils to face, by land and fea,
    That tongue can never tell ye?
And wilt thou all thefe dangers fcorn,
    Whilft in thefe arms
    I hold thy charms,
Enraptur'd ev'ry opening morn,
    When the drum beats reveillez.

FANNY.

Yes, yes, Platoon—I'll go with thee
In danger, whatfoe'er it be—
    Believe 'tis truth I tell you:
My conftant mind fhall peril fcorn,
    Brave all alarms,
    So in my arms
I hold thee every opening morn,
    When the drum beats leveillez.

PLATOON.

Still Fanny wilt thou go with me?
Suppofe the cruel fates decree,
    Alas how fhall I tell you?
The news fhould come—thy foldier fell,
    And thou fha't hear,
    Appall'd with fear,
Next morning his fatal paffing bell,
    When the drum beats reveillez.

FANNY.

Still fearlefs will I go with thee,.
Refign'd to cruel fate's decree,
    And bravely this I tell you:
When on the fpot my foldier fell
    I'd fhed a tear,
    The world fhould hear,
Mingling with his, my paffing bell,
    When the drum beats reveillez.

BOTH.

To the world's end I'd go with thee,
Where thou art, danger ne'er can be;
    My joy no tongue can tell ye:

And fure fuch love may perils fcorn,
    Brave all alarms,
    While in my arms
I hold thee every op'ning morn,
    When the drum beats reveillez.

BALLAD.

NOSEGAYS I cry, and, though little you pay,
'They are fuch as you cannot get every day.
Who'll buy,? who'll buy?—'tis nofegays I cry.
Who'll buy? who'll buy?—'tis nofegays I cry.
    Each mincing, ambling, lifping blade,
    Who fmiles, and talks of bliffes
    He never felt, is here portray'd
    In form of a Narciffes.
        Nofegays I cry, &c.

Statefmen, like Indians, who adore
    The fun, by courting power,
Cannot be fhewn their likenefs more
    Than in th' humble fun-flower.
        Nofegays I cry, &c.

Poets I've here in fprigs of bays,
    Devils in the bufh are friars;
Nettles are critics, who damn plays,
    And fatirifts are briars.
        Nofegays I cry, &c.

BALLAD—IN TOM THUMB.

THE younker, who his firft effay
    Makes in the front of battle.
Stands all aghaft, while cohorns play,
    And bullets round him rattle
Put pride fteps in, and now no more
  · Feil fear his jav'lin lances,
Like dulcet flutes the cannons roar,
    And groans turn country dances

So frights, and flurries, and what not,
    Upon my fancy ruflics,
I fear I know not why or what,
    I'm cover'd o'er with blufhes,

But let the honey feafon fly,
  To fecond well my clapper,
The kitchen's whole artillery
  Shall grace my hufband's napper.

BALLAD—IN THE WHIM OF THE MOMENT.

'TIS faid we venturous die-hards, when we leave the fhore,
  Our friends fhould mourn,
  Left we return'
To blefs their fight no more :
  But this is all a notion
    Bold Jack can't underftand,
  Some die upon the ocean,
    And fome on the land :
    Then fince 'tis clear,
    Howe'er we fteer,
No man's life's under his command.
    Let tempefts howl,
    And billows roll,
  And dangers prefs :
Of thofe in fpight, there are fome joys
  Us jolly tars to blefs,
For Saturday night ftill comes my boys,
  To drink to Poll and Befs.

One feaman hands the fail, another heaves the log,
  The purfer fwops
  Our pay for flops,
The landlord fells us grog ;
  Then each man to his ftation,
    To keep life's fhip in trim,
  What argufies noration ?
    The reft is all a whim :
    Cheerly my hearts,
    Then play your parts,
Boldly refolved to fink or fwim ;
    The mighty furge
    May ruin urge,
Of thofe in fpight, &c.

For all the world juft like the ropes aboard a fhip,
  Each man's rigg'd out
  A veffel ftout,
To take for life a trip :

The shrouds, the stays, and braces
Are joys, and hopes, and fears,
The halliards, sheets and traces,
Still, as each passion veers,
And whim prevails,
Direct the sails,
As on the sea of life he steers:
Then let the storm
Heaven's face deform,
And danger press:
Of those in spight, &c.

────── ◇ ──◇── ◈ ◈ ◈ ──◀── ◀◇── •

BALLAD—IN THE WHIM OF THE MOMENT.

THE grey-ey'd Aurora, in saffron array,
"Twixt my curtains in vain took a peep,
And though broader and broader still brightened the day,
Nought could wake me, so sound did I sleep.
At length rosy Phœbus look'd full in my face,
Full and fervent but nothing would do,
Till the dogs yelp'd impatient, and long'd for the chase,
And shouting appear'd the whole crew.
Come on, yoics honies, hark forward my boys,
There ne'er was so charming a morn,
Follow, follow, wake Echo, to share in our joys—
Now the music, now echo—mark! mark!
Hark! hark!
The silver-mouth'd hounds, and the mellow ton'd horn.
Fresh as that smiling morn from which they drew breath,
My companions are rang'd on the plain,
Blest with rosy contentment, that nature's best wealth,
Which monarchs aspire to in vain:
Now spirits like fire every bosom invade,
And now we in order set out,
While each neighb'ring valley, rock, woodland, and glade,
Re-vollies the air-rending shout.
        Come on, &c.

Now renard's unearth'd, and runs fairly in view,
Now we've lost him so subtily he turns,
But the scent lies so strong, still we fearless pursue,
While each object impatiently burns:
Hark! Babler gives tongue, and Fleet, Driver, and Sly,
The fox now the covert forsakes,
Again he's in view, let us after him fly,
Now, now to the river he takes.
        Come on, &c.

From the river poor renard can make but one puſh,
  No longer ſo proudly he flies,
Tir'd, jaded, worn out, we are cloſe to his bruſh,
  And conqer'd, like Cæſar, he dies.
And now in high glee to board we repair,
  Where fat, as we jovially quaff,
His portion of merit let every man ſhare,
  And promote the convivial laugh.
    Come on, &c.

BALLAD—IN THE WHIM OF THE MOMENT.

FROM prudence let my joys take birth,
  Let me not be paſſion's ſlave,
Approv'd by reaſon, ſweet's the mirth,
  Vice of pleaſure is the grave.
Then ſtill to reaſon's dictates true,
  Select the ſweets of life like bees;
Thus your enjoyments will be few
  But ſuch as on reflection pleaſe.

Wine exhilirates the ſoul,
  Inſpires the mirth of every feaſt,
But gluttons ſo may drain the bowl,
  Till man degenerates to beaſt :
Then mirth and wiſdom keep in view,
  And freely on the bottle ſeize ;
What though your pleaſures are but few !
  They're ſuch as on reflection pleaſe.

Love the ſource of human joys,
  The mind with bliſs that ſweetly fills,
Too often its own end deſtroys,
  And proves the ſource of human ills.
Here reaſon's dictates keep in view,
  Or, farewell freedom, farewell eaſe,
The real joys of life are few
  But ſuch as on reflection pleaſe.

Then while we meet, let's only own
  Joys that do honor to the heart,
And ceaſing to prize theſe alone,
  Deplore our frailty, ſigh, and part ;
Meanwhile to reaſon's dictates true,
  Select the ſweets of life like bees,
Thus your enjoyments will be few
  But ſuch as on reflection pleaſe.

www.ingramcontent.com/pod-product-compliance
Lightning Source LLC
Chambersburg PA
CBHW021531270326
41930CB00008B/1201